The Egyptians

ROSEMARY REES

Heinemann

First published in Great Britain by
Heinemann Library
an imprint of Heinemann Publishers
(Oxford) Ltd
Halley Court, Jordan Hill, Oxford OX2 8EJ

OXFORD LONDON EDINBURGH MADRID
ATHENS BOLOGNA PARIS MELBOURNE
SYDNEY AUCKLAND SINGAPORE TOKYO
IBADAN NAIROBI HARARE GABORONE
PORTSMOUTH NH (USA)

98 97 96 95 94
10 9 8 7 6 5 4 3 2 1

British Library Cataloguing in Publication Data is available from the British Library on request.

ISBN 0 431 07803 3 (hardback)
    0 431 07780 0 (paperback)

Designed by Ron Kamen, Green Door
Design Ltd, Basingstoke

Printed in China   00338 1501

Photographic acknowledgements
The author and publishers wish to
acknowledge with thanks the following
photographic sources:

a = above b = below l = left r = right

By courtesy of the Trustees of the British
Museum 23*l*, 31*r*, 33*l*, 36; C M Dixon 9, 21,
22, 24, 25*r*, 28*r*, 31*l*, 35, 37–39, 51*l*, 52, 54,
58; E T Archive 10, 12, 27*a*, 55, 56; Werner
Forman Archive 8, 14, 26, 27*b*, 28*l*, 42*l*, 44,
48*r*, 49, 50, 53*l*; Michael Holford 5, 7, 13,
17*l*, 18, 20, 23*r*, 25*l*, 29, 34, 40*l*, 41, 43, 45,
46*l*, 48*l*, 51*r*, 54*br*, 57*l*, 59; Hutchison Library
6, 30, 40*r*, 46*r*; William Macquitty 11*l*, 17*r*,
33*r*, 42*r*, National Center for
Supercomputing Applications 11*r*.

The publishers have made every effort to
trace the copyright holders, but if they
have inadvertently overlooked any, they
will be pleased to make the necessary
arrangement at the first opportunity.

Cover photograph © British Museum

Note to the reader – In this book there are some words in the text which are printed in **bold** type. This shows that the word is lited in the glossary on page 62. The glossary gives a brief explanation of words which may be new to you.

Contents

Who were the Egyptians?

About 5000 years ago a new way of life grew up along the banks of the river Nile in Egypt. It lasted for over 3000 years. This is longer than any other **civilization** in the history of the world. Experts know more about the ancient Egyptians than they do about the ancient Greeks or Romans. This is because a great number of buildings and objects made by the ancient Egyptians can still be seen today.

A mixture of peoples
The people who settled in Egypt came from many different places. The red arrows on the map below show where they came from.

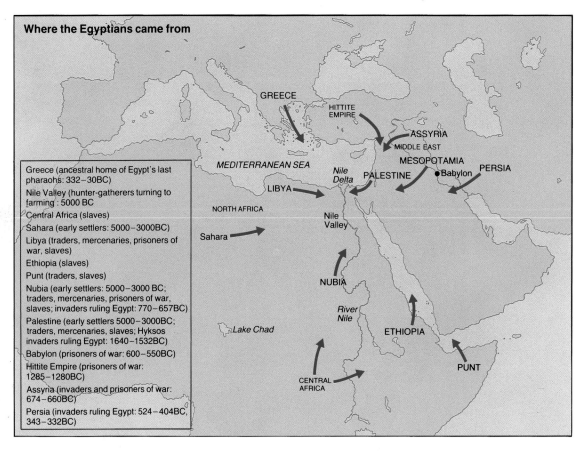

Where the Egyptians came from

Greece (ancestral home of Egypt's last pharaohs: 332–30BC)

Nile Valley (hunter-gatherers turning to farming : 5000 BC)

Central Africa (slaves)

Sahara (early settlers: 5000–3000BC)

Libya (traders, mercenaries, prisoners of war, slaves)

Ethiopia (slaves)

Punt (traders, slaves)

Nubia (early settlers: 5000–3000 BC; traders, mercenaries, prisoners of war, slaves; invaders ruling Egypt: 770–657BC)

Palestine (early settlers 5000–3000BC; traders, mercenaries, slaves; Hyksos invaders ruling Egypt: 1640–1532BC)

Babylon (prisoners of war: 600–550BC)

Hittite Empire (prisoners of war: 1285–1280BC)

Assyria (invaders and prisoners of war: 674–660BC)

Persia (invaders ruling Egypt: 524–404BC, 343–332BC)

This is a photograph of the Great Sphinx. It is guarding the stone pyramid you can see in the background. An Egyptian ruler, the **pharaoh** Khephren, was buried in the pyramid about 4500 years ago. Egyptians dug the Great Sphinx out of the sand about 2400 years ago. They did not know, and no one knows now, why the sphinx has the head of a man and the body of a lion.

The early Egyptians

The very first people who lived by the river Nile lived mainly by hunting for meat and gathering wild plants. They kept some cows, sheep and goats. They grew a few crops.

The Egyptians grew flax, barley and a kind of wheat called emmer. These plants did not grow wild in the Nile valley. They had first been used by farmers in the Middle East. This means that some of the first Egyptian farmers probably came from the Middle East. However, the language, religion and art that grew up in Egypt were very different from that of the Middle East. Many **historians** believe that most of the early farming people came from North Africa.

Dates from long ago
Almost all of the dates in this book are BC dates. They count the number of years *before* the birth of Christ. When dates are given for things that have happened *since* the birth of Christ, the letters AD come in front of the year. When historians are not sure about a date it is printed in this book with a question mark.

The gift of the Nile

Seven thousand years ago the Nile valley was mostly a swamp. Fewer than 30 000 people were able to live there, hunting animals and gathering crops. Land in other parts of the Middle East was far more fertile. Farmers in Mesopotamia grew a lot of food. They used **dikes** and **irrigation** canals to control the flood water from their rivers. This made the soil rich and **fertile**. More and more people were able to live there because there was enough food for them.

This is the River Nile today. Only the land along the banks of the Nile is rich and fertile. Almost no rain falls on Egypt. The country still depends on the Nile for almost all of its water.

Egypt becomes fertile

Gradually the climate everywhere became drier. Less rain was falling in the African lands, far to the south, that fed water to the Nile. The level of the river fell. As it fell, a strip of rich, black land emerged along each of its banks. This was fertile soil. Every year the Nile flooded. Every year there was more rich, fertile soil. It was this soil that helped make Egypt such a great country. Eventually, 2000 years ago, more than eight million people lived and worked in the Nile valley.

Egyptians painted these pictures on a scroll. They buried the scroll with an important official called Nakht. It shows what the Egyptians hoped for in life after death. They hoped for fertile fields surrounded by water.

The Black Land

'The Black Land' was the Egyptians' name for their country. This was because the fertile land along the Nile (shown in dark green) was black.
On each side of the river were the 'Red Lands'. These were deserts. No one lived there. They protected the Black Lands from invasion by Egypt's enemies. So did the **cataracts** and rapids south of Egypt on the Nile.
Travel across the desert was difficult. This meant the Egyptians could not easily defend their **oases**. The Faiyum Oasis was the only one the Egyptians controlled all the time. This was because it was near to the River Nile and could be defended easily. The Egyptian **pharaohs** moved their troops by water up and down the Nile to meet their enemies who could only advance slowly across land.

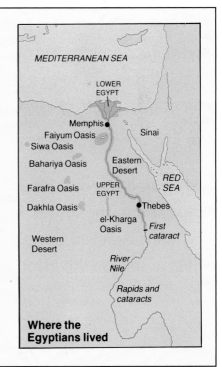

Where the Egyptians lived

How do we know about the Egyptians?

About 300 people all over the world spend their time finding out about the Egyptians. They work in museums and universities . They are called **Egyptologists**.

Looking underneath the ground

Archaeologists are people who have been specially trained to **excavate** and uncover ruins of old buildings. They also find everyday objects (called artefacts) made by people in the past. From these they build up a picture of the past and how people lived.

Archaeologists found homes on the edge of the desert which were lived in by ancient Egyptians. Remains of really ancient houses on the banks of the Nile have not been found, because they were swept away when the Nile flooded.

Archaeologists found the tombs of important Egyptians. In the tombs was everything the Egyptians believed that the person needed in order to survive life after death.

This is a wooden statue from the tombs at Sakkara. It is probably a priest, and is definitely more than 4400 years old. The wood has not rotted at all because Egypt's climate is so hot and dry. All that has gone is the paint that originally covered the statue. In wetter countries the statue would have rotted away.

Looking at stones and papers

Some Egyptian tombs are under the ground. Others, such as the pyramids, are above ground and can be seen clearly. Archaeologists had to find a way in. They had to hope that grave robbers had not been there before them, thousands of years ago. Many temples, too, are still standing. Their carvings and statues tell us about the pharaohs and about Egyptian beliefs. We also know about Egypt through thousands of **papyrus** letters and documents that have survived in Egypt's dry air.

The golden mask of Tutankhamon
Tutankhamon was an unimportant pharaoh whose burial chamber was not robbed before it could be studied. Archaeologists found wonderful treasures there. This shows that more important pharaohs must have been surrounded by even greater treasures.

We know about Egyptian learning through writings on papyrus scrolls. This is part of a papyrus scroll. It was written in about 650BC. It is a copy of a much older scroll.

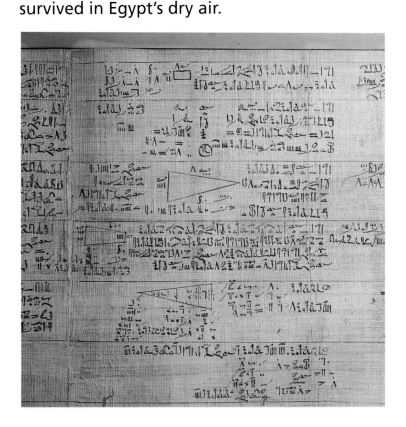

Looking after Egypt's past

In AD1954 archaeologists were working near the base of the Great Pyramid of Khufu at Giza in Egypt. They found a sealed room. When they opened the room the air inside escaped. That ancient air had been trapped inside for 4600 years. The archaeologists wished they had been able to analyse the air. They might have been able to find out something more about ancient Egypt. In AD1987 archaeologists tried to capture some ancient air from a room nearby which they thought was sealed in the same way. When they pumped the air out, however, it smelled stale. The sealed room had been damaged. The air was not ancient at all. This shows us how difficult it is to study ancient **sites** without losing or destroying some evidence from the past.

Scientific archaeology

In the past a lot of information was lost because people just took objects from sites and gave them to museums. Now archaeologists make very careful notes of where every find is discovered.

Wall paintings tell us a lot about the lives of ancient Egyptians. The problem is that old paint fades very quickly. Nowadays archaeologists take photographs of the paintings they discover. Before photography, the paintings were copied. Giovanni Belzoni copied this painting from a tomb wall in Thebes. Many of the actual wall paintings he copied have faded away. As well as copying paintings, he sent many treasures to the British Museum.

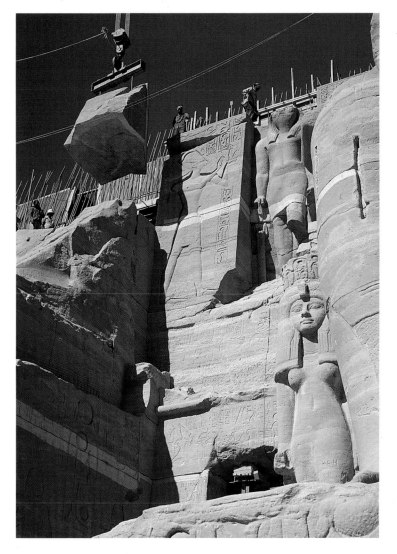

Moving a temple out of harm's way
This ancient temple at Abu Simbel is being moved. If it stayed put it would have been under water when a new dam was built. These workmen have cut and are now lifting stones very carefully.

Looking without disturbing
Scientists used X-rays and computers to make this three-dimensional image of an unknown Egyptian's head. If they had unwrapped the body (called a mummy) it would not have lasted long.

Archaeologists know that every clue is important in putting together the story of the past. One problem is that many ancient objects fade and crumble when they get into the light and air. Scientists can now preserve objects that have been in the ground for a long time.

Pictures and picture writing

When Egyptians painted pictures they were not trying to show what people really looked like. A picture was a kind of diagram. Egyptians believed that their pictures had magical powers. For example, they made the picture painting on page 7 as a **charm** to help the dead nobleman's spirit feed itself in the **afterlife**.

Pictures like writing
This is part of a funeral stone. The artist has followed many rules in making the pictures and the writing. For example, the man is facing right. The woman is facing left. This means the man is more important than the woman. When two people face each other, the more important person always faces right.

Hieroglyphics

Egyptians sometimes wrote in pictures. This sort of writing is called **hieroglyphics**. The Egyptians invented it about 5000 years ago (around 3000BC). The Egyptians believed that hieroglyphics were magical, too. They used them mostly in temples and in tombs.

Hieratic writing

There are thousands of pieces of everyday papyrus letters, official reports and essays. They tell us that the Egyptians told jokes, complained, quarrelled and sometimes behaved badly. Thieves robbed and judges took bribes; officials and generals plotted against their pharaohs; soldiers, peasants and slaves ran away from their masters. These ordinary writings were in **hieratic script**, which did not use pictures and which could be written much more quickly than hieroglyphics. The Egyptians also used **demotic script**, which was a simple form of hieratic script. Demotic script was carved on the Rosetta Stone.

Horus   b-j-k (hawk)

Spelling
All hieroglyphic symbols began as pictures. One picture stood for one whole word. This symbol of a hawk stood for the god Horus. Word pictures also worked as signs for sounds. These signs spelled the word 'hawk'.

The Rosetta Stone
The same information was carved in hieroglyphics (top), **demotic script** (middle) and Greek (bottom). Jean Francois Champollion understood Greek and used it to work out the other languages.

The pharaoh kings of Egypt

The word '**pharaoh**' means 'the one who lives in the palace'. The Egyptian pharaoh kings had a long list of more official titles. The Egyptians believed that no single name could describe the greatness of their rulers. They called their pharaohs by the names of their gods.

The royal dynasties

A pharaoh usually had more than one wife. One of the wives was the 'great royal queen'. Egyptians believed this wife had two special blessings. One was from Isis, who was the first goddess-queen of Egypt. The other was from Hathor, the goddess of women. Usually a son of the great royal queen became pharaoh when his father died.

A line of rulers who pass on their throne from one member of their family to another over many, many years is called a **dynasty**. Sometimes dynasties died out. Sometimes they were overthrown by foreign conquerors. Over 3000 years 31 different dynasties ruled Egypt.

Before the first pharaohs, many kings fought for control of different parts of the Nile valley. In this carving King Narmer of **Upper Egypt** is killing an enemy prisoner.

Crown of Upper Egypt   Crown of Lower Egypt   Crown of all Egypt   War crown   Hemhemet crown

The pharaohs of 3000 years

Egyptologists have tried to work out when particular pharaohs ruled and when certain dynasties began and ended. They do this by studying the lists made by historians at the time of the ancient Egyptians. Some ancient **scrolls** mention comets and the position of stars. Modern **astronomy** can tell us when these comets and stars appeared in ancient times. Egyptologists can then work out more accurately when certain pharaohs ruled.

Egyptian dynasties are grouped by periods. The time before the pharaohs is called the **predynastic period**. The time of the first pharaohs is called the **early period**. The most important periods as far as the pharaohs were concerned are called kingdoms.

Predynastic period	5000–3100BC (?)
Early period	3100–2649BC (?)
Old Kingdom	2649–2134BC (?)
Middle Kingdom	2040–1640BC (?)
New Kingdom	1550–1070BC (?)

Crowns of the pharaohs
The pharoah kings of Egypt wore these crowns on different occasions.

Sedge   Bee

Two words for king
A sedge was the Lower Egyptian sign for royalty; a bee was the Upper Egyptian sign. These are the hieroglyphics for them.

The pharaohs and the gods

The Egyptians spoke to their pharaoh as if he was a god. In fact, they gave him the names of several gods. His official title included names such as Re, who was the sun-god and Egypt's chief god. His title also included the names Horus, the god with the head of a hawk; Nakhbet, who protected **Upper Egypt**; and Wadjet, who protected **Lower Egypt**.

When a pharaoh died, the name of the god Osiris was carved on his tomb. Osiris was the god of the **Underworld**, a place where all good Egyptians went to when they died.

This is the title of the pharaoh Thotmes IV, written in hieroglyphics.

Horus   Nakhbet and Wadjet   Golden Horus

Re is everlasting   Son of Re   Thotmes   Beloved of Amon-Re   Giver of life like Re

The official title of the pharaoh Thotmes IV includes several godlike names. The name Thotmes itself is treated as godlike by enclosing it in an oblong frame called a **cartouche** just as the godly phrase 'Re is everlasting' is enclosed.

The cartouche symbolizes the everlasting cycle of the sun-god's journey across the heavens by day and beneath the Earth by night .

The story of Osiris

Osiris was the god-king of Egypt. His brother Seth cut Osiris' body into pieces. Seth scattered the pieces up and down the Nile, so he could seize the country for himself. Isis found the pieces and put them back together. Osiris became king of the Underworld. Horus, the son of Osiris and Isis, fought with Seth for the throne of Egypt. The gods approved of Horus and he became the rightful king. By calling their pharaoh 'Horus' the Egyptians were saying that he was their rightful king.

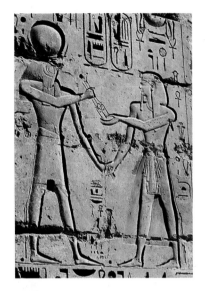

Giver of life
This is a wall carving in a temple. The god Re is giving an anhk to the pharaoh. An ankh is the hieroglyphic symbol for life.

Osiris, king of the Underworld
In this picture a dead soul is giving gifts to the god Osiris.

17

The pyramid-builders

The Egyptians built pyramids to hold the tombs of their pharaohs. Archaeologists have so far discovered 46 pyramids. There may well be more, lying under the desert sands.

Leading the world in stonework

Pyramids are the first buildings made by precisely cutting and putting together great blocks of stone. In this, the Egyptians led the world for 2000 years.

The **Step Pyramid** looks like this today. The drawing below shows what it looked like when it was first built. It was the very first pyramid. It was built for the pharaoh Zoser by his great scribe Imhotep.

A true pyramid had smooth sides and came to a point. This is a drawing of the pyramid at Abusir. It was finished more than 4400 years ago.

How were the pyramids built? Probably the work gangs built huge ramps of sand and hauled the great stones up them over rollers.

Why the pyramids were built

Before the pyramids, Egyptians buried their pharaohs in **mastabas**. These were long, low buildings made from bricks or small stones.

Zoser (2630–2611BC) was one of the first pharaohs of the Old Kingdom. When he died the Egyptians decided to put his body in a pyramid. They decided that this pyramid should rise by steps so that Zoser's spirit could climb to meet the sun. Later, the Egyptians build pyramids with smooth sides. The Egyptians built most of their pyramids near Memphis, which was the capital of ancient Egypt. It is not far from Cairo, the modern capital.

Inside a pyramid Pyramids were mostly filled with stones and rubble. There were also passageways leading to the burial chamber of the pharaoh. Sometimes the Egyptians built false chambers and passageways which led nowhere. This was to confuse grave-robbers.

Death and life after death

Egyptians believed that, at the end of every day, the sun-god Re died in the western sky at sunset. Everyone in Egypt prayed for his return. Re was re-born every morning at sunrise.

The Egyptians believed that, when Re died each evening, he went down into the Underworld. This was a perfect place which brought Re back to life as he journeyed through it. The Egyptians believed they, too, could reach this world if their bodies were preserved when they died.

Funeral ceremonies
In this picture four priests are opening the mummy's mouth with a specially shaped stick. This is so that he can eat in the afterlife.

The judgement of the gods
The god of mummification, Anubis, is weighing a dead man's heart. The heart is on one side of the balance; a feather, representing truth, is on the other. If the scales do not balance, monsters would come and eat the dead man's soul.

Making a home for a spirit

The Egyptians made a dead person's body into a **mummy** which would never decay. They believed that this gave a lasting home to the person's **ka**, or body-spirit. The person's soul, or **ba**, could move through the Underworld and return to Earth, so long as the ka survived.

The Egyptians mummified their pharaohs and put them in unchanging tombs of stone – the pyramids. Wealthy Egyptians made their own arrangements to be mummified. People who were too poor to afford this hoped that their ba would join the 'boat of millions'. This was a golden ship full of good souls in which Re crossed and re-crossed the sky.

A tombstone inscription
Most Egyptian tombstones were like this one. It reminded the living that they should make offerings to Osiris, the god of the Underworld. They should do this on behalf of the dead.

Hathor, goddess of women and trees
She is pouring water to quench the thirst of a dead woman's ka and ba.

Mummies and medicines

The Egyptians thought that the dead needed their bodies as much as the living did. A person's soul needed somewhere to live after death. This is why they preserved people's bodies when they died.

Making a mummy

Caring for bodies was the work of priests. The priests made a dead body into a mummy. They learned, by making mummies, how bodies work.

Making a mummy naturally
This Egyptian died about 5000 years ago. The desert sand dried and preserved his body. The clay pots were there because the Egyptians thought he might need them in his next life.

Visiting the doctor

Most priests were doctors, too. They prescribed medicines. Some of the medicines were made from herbs. Treatments for illnesses could involve **sacrifices** to the gods, spells and wearing charms. Some priest-doctors set bones skilfully, and bandaged wounds.

Egyptian ideas spread to Greece

In the winter of 332–331BC Alexander the Great conquered Egypt. Egypt became part of the Greek Empire. Alexander set up a new city, Alexandria. Here the Greeks started a university and a library. They gathered together all the knowledge they could find from Egypt. Egyptian knowledge and understanding about **anatomy** and **disease** spread all over the Greek Empire.

Making mummies
This mummy is a priestess from Thebes. She died in about 1000 BC. When she was dead, priests covered her body in natron. This is a chemical made from salt. The natron drew water out of the body and so dried it. Then priests wrapped the mummy in **linen** bandages.

Canopic jars
Priests put a person's liver, intestines, stomach and lungs into these special jars.

Temples and their gods

Egyptians worshipped over 2000 gods. Most of them were local spirits who controlled a particular hill or tree. At that place people built a small **shrine** out of mud bricks or matting. They put a clay model of the spirit inside. This was the home on Earth of the spirit. People prayed at the shrine and asked for favours. A few gods were great gods who were worshipped all over Egypt. Their images, made by the best craftsmen, were housed in golden shrines kept in stone temples.

Priests

Priests had to be very clean for the gods they served. Some of them shaved all the hair from their bodies. Others bathed in sacred pools. Ordinary priests could only do basic jobs like sweeping out the temple.

In the inner sanctuary was a golden shrine. Inside the shrine was a beautiful statue. The god of the temple was supposed to live in the statue. Every morning the senior priests broke the clay seal on the sanctuary door and brought the god out for worship.

Amon-Re
This is a statue of the sun-god in the shape of Amon. The statue is almost 3000 years old. It is made of solid silver and covered with gold.

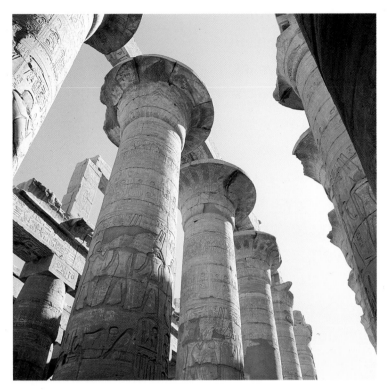

The ruins of the temple of Amon at Karnak, near Thebes
These columns once supported the roof. The columns are so huge that 100 people could stand on the top of one of them. This temple was especially rich. It had magnificent buildings and many full-time priests.

Priestesses

Only a few women became priestesses. However, the high-priestess of Amon was the most holy person in the whole of the area around Thebes, apart from the pharaoh.

Gods of the pharaohs

The pharaohs joined the names of similar gods into one. For example, the sun-god Re was called Re-Harakhty or Amon-Re, depending on whether the town of Harakhty or Amon was the more powerful at the time.

Animal-headed gods
Some gods had the heads of animals. The Egyptians believed that some animals were closely connected to magical powers. Animals, especially the cat, were worshipped in many temples.

How was Egypt governed?

The pharaoh of Egypt was an **absolute ruler**. He did not have to obey any laws himself. He could change any laws he wanted. However, to rule well a pharaoh needed help from other people. He would have had a very difficult time if important people such as priests, generals and landowners thought that he was offending the gods. They might think this if he changed too many laws or did not look after the needs of Egypt.

The pharaoh had to let other people decide some things for him. He could not be everywhere, making all the decisions. Most of his decisions were made by the **scribes**.

Scribes, generals and priests

The younger sons of landowners and nobles trained to be scribes. The most wealthy of them went to the great school for scribes at Thebes. They learned history, poetry, surveying, architecture and accountancy. Most of them went into the pharaoh's service as government officials.

Scribes
Scribes like this ran Egypt. They worked in mud-brick offices in small villages along the banks of the river Nile. They collected taxes, settled legal arguments, worked as priests, designed and organized the construction of public buildings and persuaded young men to join the army in time of war.

Taxes

This model of a servant was buried with a rich man. He was ready to do whatever the gods of the Underworld asked from his master. The gods demanded taxes in the Underworld in the same way as the pharaohs did in life. A living Egyptian paid his taxes by sending servants to work for the pharaoh. What would a dead Egyptian do in the Underworld?

The pharaoh's closest advisors were scribes belonging to Egypt's most important families. One scribe, the **vizier**, became the pharaoh's prime minister.

Women scribes

Very few women learned to read and write in ancient Egypt. However, the Egyptians had a feminine word for scribe, so we know that some scribes must have been women. We know very little about them.

Women rulers

Egypt was ruled at least three times by women:

Nefrusobk   1787–1783BC
Hatshepsut   1473–1458BC(?)
Twosre   1198–1196BC(?)

Nefertiti, the great royal queen of the pharaoh Akhnaton, took a very active part in his reign (1353–1335BC(?)).

During the **Greek period** (332–30BC) Greek-speaking queens such as Arsinoe, Berenice and Cleopatra ruled Egypt. They did this either by themselves or with their husbands.

Cleopatra VII, the last Greek-speaking queen

What did the Egyptians wear?

Egypt is a hot country. The people did not wear many clothes. What they did wear, however, mattered a great deal. It showed how rich they were. It showed what their position was in society.

Men's clothes

Men usually wore a skirt, or **kilt**. A peasant's kilt was made from rough cloth and was tucked up to keep his legs free when he worked in the fields. A noble's kilt was long and made from fine **linen**.

An important official and his wife
Their clothes are made from fine linen. The man's necklace and plaited hair show that he has an important job. This statue was made from limestone in about 2550BC.

Children
Most children wore no clothes at all. These boys came from a rich family. You can tell this because their hair has been carefully tied into side locks. Servants would have done this for them. The very youngest children had their heads shaved.

Women's clothes

Peasant women wore dresses made from rough cloth. Wealthy women wore dresses made from fine linen. They were usually bleached white, but some were dyed orange, yellow or green. The best dresses were pleated.

Make-up and hairstyles

Women wore green or black eye make-up. On special occasions men used eye make-up to outline their eyes.

Women usually had long hair. Poor women sold their hair to wig-makers. Rich women bought the wigs, which were made in elaborate hair-styles. They wore them on special occasions.

Fine clothes
This man and his wife are wearing linen dresses. The cloth is so finely woven that you can see through it. The woman has a cone of animal fat on top of her head. It melts slowly into her hair and makes it smell nice.

Glazed ceramic jewellery
This jewellery was made 2500 years ago. It was everyday jewellery for a rich woman. Peasant women wore beads, but their beads were rough. On special occasions rich women wore lotus flowers, gold rings, earrings, necklaces, bracelets and anklets.

An Egyptian village

Most Egyptians in ancient times lived in villages. The only towns were Memphis and Thebes. The Egyptians built their villages on the banks of canals or rivers. They used boats when they needed to travel to another village.

Villagers were usually hard at work. Most men were in the fields looking after crops and animals. Only the craftsmen would stay in the village to work. Most of the village women spent their time weaving. Small children played naked in the streets. Older children helped their parents.

A modern Egyptian village near Luxor
This modern village looks very like an ancient one. Ancient Egyptian villages were just a cluster of flat-topped houses built from mud bricks. The houses were built along narrow streets leading from the market-place. Most houses had two or three rooms.

The village market

Market days were always very busy occasions. People came from the villages up and down river. Local craftsmen and peasant women laid out goods to sell on cloths which they spread on the ground. There was food and drink for sale: salt, barley, onions, peas, beans, barley bread and beer. People liked to buy fish from the River Nile, fresh, salted or dried. Craftsmen sold what they had made. This could be, for example, woven wicker baskets, leather, jewellery or clay pots. Magicians would also be there, selling medical advice and magic charms to protect the villagers from evil.

People used donkeys to carry anything heavy. Dogs and pigs rooted around trying to find tasty bits of food that had been thrown out.

Landowners and senior scribes had large homes on the edges of villages. Their homes were surrounded by high walls. Sometimes really important people had houses that stood apart from the villages.

A village house
This clay model of a village house was found in a tomb. It is of a craftsman's house. His workshops are on the ground floor and his living rooms are above.

A village market scene
The villagers are going to be able to buy some fresh beef.

What were Egyptians' homes like?

Archaeologists have not been able to excavate many Egyptian homes. This is because the floodwaters of the Nile swept most of them away. However, in the desert near the royal tombs, the ancient Egyptians built some special villages. These were for workmen and craftsmen to live in while they worked on the tombs.

A craftsman's house

The desert houses were built side by side along a street. They were long and narrow, as you can see from the drawing.

Inside a craftsman's home
This is a modern drawing of the inside of a craftsman's house. It was built 3500 years ago at Deir el-Medina near Thebes.

Vent · Roof fence · Door to bedroom · Palm logs and thatch · Workroom · Mud-brick oven · Open-air kitchen · Birth shrine · Pillar · Shrine · Cellar · Cellar

Part of the front room was bricked off to make a shrine. Here the family left food for their **ancestors**. Babies were born here. The parents hoped that the ancestors would make sure that no wicked souls were born into the family. The next room was the main one in the house. Small windows high in the wall let in light. There were mud benches around the walls. In the walls there were shrines to gods. Two narrow rooms came next. One was a bedroom with sleeping mats on the floor. The other was a room where the craftsmen worked. Steps at the back led up to the roof. The family ate their evening meal here and sometimes slept here. The kitchen, too, was outdoors, in a yard at the back of the house.

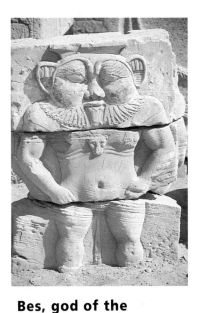

Bes, god of the household
Every home had a shrine with the image of Bes in it. He was the protector of women and god of childbirth.

Bedroom furniture
The Egyptians stretched canvas across the bed frame and slept on it. Instead of a pillow they used a headrest, which you can see on the floor at the back of the frame.

Family life

Most of what we know about Egyptian life has been told to us by Egyptian men. They were mainly interested in what men did. They do give us glimpses, however, of what life was like for women and children.

Husbands and wives

Powerful men, such as the pharaoh, had more than one wife. Most men, had only one.

Nebamon and his family
This is a painting from Nebamon's tomb. It shows him hunting birds in the marshes. Can you find his wife and daughter? Egyptians painted the people they thought were less important smaller than important people.

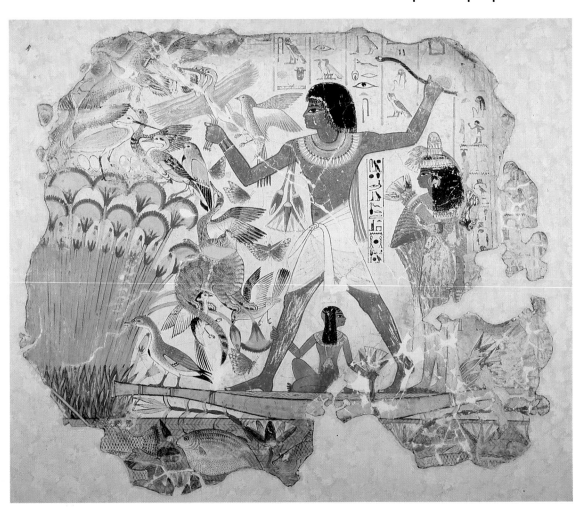

The cat

Egyptians believed that cats were sacred. They believed that male cats represented the sun, and female cats the goddess Bast. All cats were supposed to be looked after by Sekhmet, the fierce goddess of war. Whole temples were devoted to cat worship. It was forbidden to take cats out of Egypt. Special commissioners were sent to other countries to buy back cats that had been smuggled away.

The mummy of a cat
This mummy was made about 3000 years ago.

Egyptian women were allowed to own property. Most women living in other countries at the same time could not do this. Archaeologists found a scroll written in 1156BC by the tax assessor for the Faiyum Oasis. It shows that about ten per cent of the land belonged to women. Women also owned the furniture in their homes.

Children

When children were small, they played and slept most of the time. In wealthy families young boys learned to read before going to the temple school. In ordinary families children did not have any education. The boys helped their fathers and the girls helped their mothers.

Hunting and boating, feasts and fun

All Egyptians enjoyed themselves. They had plenty of fun in their spare time. Most of what we know about their spare time comes from tomb paintings of rich people.

Children

Children played tug-of-war and leap frog. Boys played at soldiers and girls played catching games with brightly coloured balls.

Feasts

Rich people held banquets. Servants offered wine and dishes of rich food to the guests. They helped themselves with their fingers. Everyone ate with their fingers. They rinsed their fingers in dishes of scented water which the servants brought round later.

A horse on wheels
This was a child's toy. Other toys were carved monkeys and wooden dolls. There were wooden cats, leopards and mice with mouths that opened and closed when children pulled a string.

Playing senet

An Egyptian noble called Ani and his wife are playing a game called senet. The rules have been lost, but archaeologists have found many senet boards and pieces. This picture was painted over 3200 years ago.

Hunting and boating

Families went hunting by boat in the marshes. Wealthy families sailed boats on the Nile. When men hunted lions they left their families behind. Hunting dogs helped to find and chase the lions. Later, the men hunted from horse-drawn chariots.

Dancing girls and musicians

Musicians were often women. As well as hand-clapping and flute playing, the women played harps, lutes and finger drums. We know what the instruments sounded like, because they have survived. We do not know what music they played, because no music was ever written down.

Cooking and eating

Food for the poor

Egyptian peasants ate mainly barley bread and onions. They made barley flour into porridge. They drank a lot of beer. Sometimes they ate fish, and, from time to time, garlic, green vegetables, dates, figs, chickpeas and lentils. Not many Egyptians ever tasted the sorts of food eaten by the rich.

Food for the rich

The rich had over 40 different kinds of bread to choose from. They were fond of roasted quails, pigeon stew, kidneys, beef ribs, fresh berries, barley cakes and cheese. They ate chicken, salted goose and wild game from the Nile marshes. They got luxury vegetables from the marshes too: wild celery, papyrus stalks and lotus root. Fishermen caught eels, mullet, carp, giant perch and tiger fish in the Nile and in the canals.

The Egyptians sometimes left cooked meals in tombs. These were for the souls of the dead. Archaeological remains of these meals, as well as tomb paintings, tell us a lot about cooking and eating.

A servant fans a charcoal cooking fire
The Egyptians did their cooking in outdoor kitchens. Kitchens were kept cool by a roof of reed matting or a thatch of palm leaves.

**Making beer
4400 years ago**
The Egyptians first mashed barley bread into a pot of water. Then they added some old beer with live yeast in it. They let the mixture stand for about a week. Then they strained off the bread and drank the liquid quickly. If they left it, the beer would soon turn into vinegar.

Grinding barley
This model was made 4000 years ago. The woman is pushing a small stone backwards and forwards over a stone slab piled with cracked barley. She is grinding the barley into flour.

The Egyptians grew grapes and made wine from them. Wine was only for the rich people.

The farming year

The Egyptians had three seasons. Each season lasted for four months. The first season was the time of the flood, called **akhet**. It lasted from August to October. Then came **peret**, the time of planting and fresh growth. From March to August was the dry season, called **shemu**, when the crops ripened and were harvested.

The season of the flood

No farming could be done while the Nile flooded. Peasants travelled to temples, shrines and markets. Villages held festivals to honour local spirits. The pharaoh's scribes ordered landowners to send peasants to work on public projects such as building pyramids or temples.

The shaduf
This is a modern photograph of a shaduf, which is still in use in Egypt today. The shaduf was used in Egypt 4000 years ago. Water for crops is lifted out of the river in a goatskin bag, which swings round onto the bank to be emptied.

Harvesting grain
Egyptians are cutting the grain with sickles. These were curved pieces of wood with sharp flints stuck into them. The men are taking away the cut grain. They are taking it to the threshing floor. There, oxen will tread on the stalks and separate them from the ears of grain.

Winnowing

After the threshing, peasants throw the grain in the air. The chaff (the light outer covering) blows away. The grains fall to the ground. Other peasants collect the grain and store it in granaries.

Sowing and reaping

The busiest time of the farming year came just after the flood. Men with wooden hoes, and cattle pulling wooden ploughs, turned over the new soil left by the flood. They dug it into the fields. Peasants scattered the seed for new crops. Then they drove a herd of cows, goats or pigs over the field. Their hooves pressed the seeds firmly into the ground.

Then the peasants could do other jobs. They repaired any damage done by the floods; they weeded and they watered the crops.

Everyone helped at harvest time. Men, women and children worked hard. They had to finish reaping before the flood covered the fields once again.

Crafts and craftsmen

Five thousand years ago, Egyptian craftsmen produced wonderfully made objects in stone, copper, gold and wood. We know this because archaeologists have found these objects in the tombs of the pharaohs. Almost all the objects were made in the same style for thousands of years. It takes a real expert to tell whether something was made 4500, 3500 or 2500 years ago.

Before the pharaohs

Egyptian **hunter-gatherers** produced the finest arrowheads and stone tools anywhere in the world. When they settled down and began farming, they made pottery and leather goods, and wove beautiful baskets.

Raised relief
This was a special sort of stone sculpture. Craftsmen cut away the stone to a depth of about 5 mm around the figures. The figures were then carved so that they stood out from the stone. Raised relief was usually used inside temples. In this scene, a pharaoh is making offerings to the sun-god Re.

Sunk relief
These figures are cut into the stone. The Egyptians usually used sunk relief outdoors, because it showed up better in sunshine.

Craftsmen at the time of the pharaohs

Craftsmen made painted stone statues and **reliefs** for temples and pyramids. They worked in groups. A senior scribe drew a plan on papyrus. It was marked on a squared grid to make copying easier. The stone or plaster was marked with the same grid, and the plan was copied onto it. Statues and reliefs were always painted, although today most of the paint has worn away. Craftsmen who painted the sculptures followed a plan on a grid, just like the sculptors did.

Craftsmanship in metal

In very early times, the Egyptians made beautiful things from copper. They made these jugs, bowls and pots from about 2300BC.

Trade and trade routes

Each Egyptian village produced all that the villagers needed to live. They produced barley, onions, lentils and bread to eat, cloth for clothes, mud bricks for building and clay pots for storage. They traded with other villages and foreigners to get more variety and better quality goods.

Trade between Egyptians

The Egyptians did not use money. Instead they took something with them to market to swap for the goods they wanted to buy. This is called **barter**. For example, a skilled craftsman might barter a carved walking stick for a sack of wheat.

The Queen of Punt
The large lady in this relief is the Queen of Punt. She had a disease that made her legs and arms swell. The rest of the relief shows a procession of men carrying gifts from the Queen of Punt to Queen Hatshepsut of Egypt. Queen Hatshepsut sent an expedition into Punt to trade for frankincense, which is used in temple rituals.

Salt was important to the Egyptians. It was sold in most village markets. Salt came from the Nile **Delta**, where sea water was left in lagoons to evaporate. Traders took the salt by boat up the Nile to village markets. Some villages specialized in luxury goods. The best pots, for example, were made in the village with the best clay. For special linen, beer or bread, Egyptians had to spend an hour or two travelling on the river.

Herbs from the land of Punt
In this relief, Queen Hatshepsut's soldiers are carrying herbs from the land of Punt. The Egyptians traded a lot of African goods, such as frankincense, with Mediterranean countries.

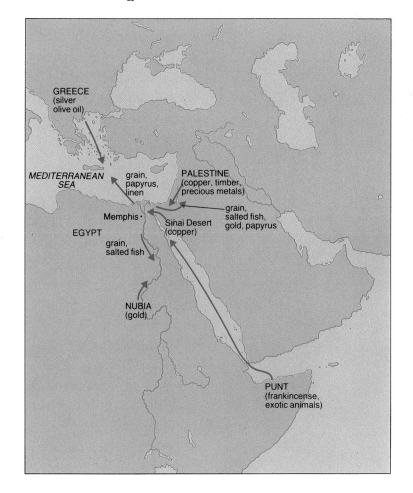

GREECE
(silver
olive oil)

MEDITERRANEAN
SEA

grain,
papyrus,
linen

PALESTINE
(copper, timber,
precious metals)

Memphis •

EGYPT

Sinai Desert
(copper)

grain,
salted fish,
gold, papyrus

grain,
salted fish

NUBIA
(gold)

PUNT
(frankincense,
exotic animals)

Trade with other countries
Egypt had grain, salted fish, ropes and papyrus scrolls which other countries needed. Egypt also had gold, which other countries wanted. Egyptian traders bartered these goods for things not found in the Nile Valley. They bartered them for wood, copper, silver and olive oil.

Travel and transport

The Egyptians could not use carts and wagons to carry goods and people long distances. This was because the wheels would just sink into the sand. They used rollers to move vast blocks of stone across the desert when they were building the pyramids, but no wagons. In 1550BC some Egyptians built the very first Egyptian vehicle with wheels. This was a war chariot.

Egyptians carried goods and people around their country by using the River Nile. They did use donkeys to carry loads to remote oases. Later they used camels. However, one boat could carry a lot more than one pack animal, and Egyptians only used animals when they had to.

A donkey
Ancient Egyptians used donkeys for short, local journeys and for carrying burdens across the desert. The first donkeys they used were not big enough for riders.

River transport
Ancient Egyptians used the River Nile to carry people and goods long distances. This boat (about 400BC) uses oars and sails to make it go extra fast.

The hieroglyphic sign for 'travelling south' was a boat with sails, because winds in Egypt blow from the north. The sign for 'travelling north' was a boat with oars.

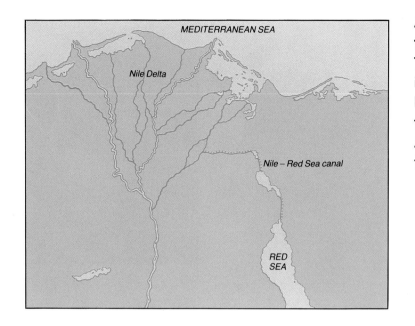

A canal from the Nile to the Red Sea
This canal was finished in 490BC. It was about 85 kilometres long. It made trading expeditions to Africa and Arabia easier for the Egyptians.

The Nile waterway

The Egyptians managed very well without wheels or camels because they had the great River Nile. The Nile carried almost everything and everyone needing to travel.

In the days before the pharaohs, Egyptians made all their boats from papyrus reeds. Later, wood from Palestine made it possible for them to build better boats. Egyptians sailed these wooden boats to Palestine, through the Red Sea and down the east coast of Africa. Fishermen and peasants carried on using small papyrus boats on local trips.

The Old Kingdom

The Egyptians began to write down their own history in about 3100BC. At about the same time, the pharaoh Menes united the kingdoms of the Nile Valley and the Nile Delta to make Egypt one country. He set up Memphis in the north and Abydos in the south as his capital cities.

The royal god, Horus the hawk
This is a statue of pharaoh Khephren (2520–2492BC) The god Horus the hawk is sitting by his shoulder. This tells the Egyptians that Khephren had the god's permission to rule.

The Great Pyramid of Khufu	
Average weight of each block	2.5 tonnes
Total number of blocks	2 300 000
Years of pharaoh Khufu's reign	23
Blocks set each year	100 000
Blocks set each day	285

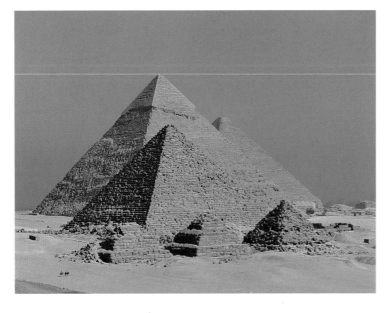

The pyramids at Giza
These pyramids are the greatest in the history of Egypt. The largest is the Great Pyramid of Khufu (2551–2528BC). Khufu taxed the Egyptian people very heavily so that he had enough money to build his pyramid.

The Old Kingdom lasted for about 500 years from 2649BC to 2134BC. The first pharaohs of the Old Kingdom did great things.

Pharaoh Zoser (2630–2611(?)BC)

Ancient Egyptians built the first pyramid ever for this pharaoh. Modern Egyptians look back to the reign of pharaoh Zoser and call it a golden age. It was a time when learning and wisdom were very important. The pharaoh's scribe, Imhotep, was a powerful man. He helped develop architecture, sculpture and medicine in Egypt.

Pharaoh Snofru (2575–2552(?)BC)

Snofru conquered part of northern Nubia. He built a lot of temples and three small pyramids. It was during his reign that worship of the sun-god Re became specially important.

The collapse of the Old Kingdom

Gradually the pharaohs lost a lot of their power. Local governors, the **nomarchs,** ruled independently. It was as though Egypt was ruled by many kings.

Pharaoh Zoser
This statue of Zoser has a battered face. Thieves damaged it thousands of years ago when they stole the jewels that were set into the eyes.

The Middle Kingdom

The pharaoh Mentuhotpe fought many battles and finally united Egypt. He called himself 'Uniter of the Two Lands' and said he was a god. People who study Egyptian history say that it was during his reign, from about 2040BC, that a new age began.

This relief shows Senwosret I with the god Ptah.

The next Mentuhotpe pharaohs

The next two pharaohs were also called Mentuhotpe. They ruled Egypt from Thebes. They opened up the Red Sea trade route and Egypt became more prosperous. Temple building began again, and the pharaohs ordered new quarries to be opened. Amon, the god of the people who lived in Thebes, became very important.

Amenhemhet I (1991–1962BC)

Amenhemhet was once the vizier (prime minister) of the last Mentuhotpe pharaoh. He became a pharaoh, and built a new capital city, Itjtawy, near Memphis.

Senwosret I (1971–1926BC)

At first, Senwosret ruled jointly with his father, Amenhemhet. They ordered many fine stone buildings to be built.

Senwosret III (1878–1841(?)BC)

Senwosret III was the greatest pharaoh of the Middle Kingdom. He kept a full-time army. His soldiers fought in Nubia and Palestine. Egypt became very powerful, and the pharaoh's government became stronger than ever before.

Queen Nefrusobk (1787–1783(?)BC)

When Senwosret III died, his officials kept the country peaceful. Gradually, however, they took more and more power for themselves. At this time Egypt had its first woman pharaoh, Queen Nefrusobk. We know almost nothing about her. Why do you think this is?

Senwosret III (1878–1841(?)BC)
This statue of Senwosret III shows him as a worried older man.

Amenhemhet III (1844–1797(?)BC)
This picture shows him destroying his enemies. In fact, his long reign was a time of peace.

The New Kingdom

In the 15th century BC the Egyptian pharaohs, who ruled from Thebes, began a struggle to expel the **Hyksos** pharaohs from Egypt. The Hyskos pharaohs ruled over people who had invaded Egypt from Palestine. They held a small area of land in the Nile Delta.

The Hyskos used bronze and iron. They fought in horse-drawn chariots. Their weapons were well designed. If the Egyptians wanted to defeat them, they had to learn a whole new technology quickly. This is just what happened. The Egyptians made chariots and weapons with the new metals. They learned to use horses. After many battles against the Hyskos, the Egyptians finally won. They ended up in charge of an united Egypt.

Amenhotep I (1525–1504(?)BC)
This pharaoh extended the Egyptian empire southwards into Nubia.

A horse-drawn war chariot
The New Kingdom began when the Egyptians from Thebes defeated the Hyksos in the Nile Delta.

Thotmes I (1504–1492(?)BC)

Thotmes I conquered Nubia, Syria and Palestine and kept them under Egyptian rule. Egypt grew strong and powerful.

Hatshepsut (1473–1458(?)BC)

Hatshepsut was a powerful queen. When her husband, Thotmes II, died, the next person to be pharaoh was only a baby. Hatshepsut ruled as **regent** for her nephew, Thotmes III. After seven years she said she was king. Thotmes III did not take charge until Hatshepsut was dead.

The next three pharaohs kept the empire strong. They gave a lot of money for temple building and to the gods to thank them for the victories that made Egypt united.

The Egyptian Empire
This map shows the Egyptian Empire when it was at its largest. The pharaoh was Thotmes I.

The funerary temple of Queen Hatshepsut
This was looked after by priests after the death of the queen. They made offerings to the gods on her behalf. Her nephew, Amenhotep III, ordered all statues of her to be destroyed. Today we do not know what she looked like.

Akhnaton

The pharaoh Amenhotep IV inherited the throne of Egypt in around 1353BC. His wife was Queen Nefertiti. Amenhotep and Nefertiti started a new religion in Egypt. This new religion was the worship of the sun-god, Aton. Because of this he changed his name to Akhnaton.

The new religion

Akhnaton wanted the Egyptians to worship only Aton. He closed the temples of all the other gods. This made their priests very angry. Akhnaton built a new capital, Akhtaton, half-way between Memphis and Thebes. At its centre was a temple without a roof, open to the sun.

Queen Nefertiti
This is a sculpture of Queen Nefertiti. She was very beautiful. She was clever, too, and influenced Akhnaton's decisions.
Below is a relief carving of Akhnaton.

Akhnaton, Nefertiti and their daughters
This relief carving was made to show the pharaoh's love for his wife and daughters. Behind them are rays of sunlight. Each ray is giving an ankh, the symbol of life, to the royal family.

Painting and sculpture

During the reign of Akhnaton, a new and different sort of art began. Artists and sculptors began showing people as they really were. They didn't paint and carve people in the traditional way. The traditional way was to make unreal pictures of people. They were supposed to look perfect, as they would look when they had reached perfection in the afterlife.

The last days of Empire

Egypt's enemies got stronger during Akhnaton's rule. Many people thought this happened because the old gods were angry. The nobles and the army remembered that when they worshipped Amon instead of Aton, they always had victories.

Tutankhamon

Tutankhamon became pharaoh after Aknhaton. He was just a boy when his rule began. His guardians moved the capital to Memphis. They changed his name from Tutankhaton to Tutankhamon to honour the old god, Amon. In these ways they hoped their luck would change, and Egypt would become powerful again.

Ramses II (1290–1224 (?)BC)

During the time of Akhnaton the Hittites took over Syria. Now, 50 years later, Ramses II fought them to a standstill in southern Syria. He made a peace with them that lasted for 50 years. He married several Hittite princesses to show he was friendly towards the Hittites.

The pharaoh Tutankhamon
Tutankhamon died when he was young. He is remembered because of the wonderful riches left in his tomb. They were never taken by robbers. We can see them in museums today.

The pharaohs lose power

Egypt gradually lost control of more and more land outside Egypt. They lost Palestine, Nubia and Syria. Inside Egypt, the priests became more and more powerful. Before long they were more powerful than the pharaohs. The temples bought more and more land and property. We know this by looking at the tax that was paid and at who paid it. In the end, the priests of Thebes ruled Upper Egypt without the pharaohs. The pharaohs controlled only the Nile Delta.

Seti I
(1305–1290(?)BC)
Seti destroyed Akhnaton's city of Akhtaton. He ordered Akhnaton's name to be taken off all carvings.

Ramses II
(1290–1224(?)BC)
He built more temples and more enormous statues of himself than any other pharaoh in history. He had hundreds of wives and more than 900 children. Egypt became poorer during his reign of 66 years.

Foreign rule

Slowly, other countries in the Middle East grew stronger. Their soldiers had iron weapons and their farmers had iron tools. They used camels to move goods and people.

The Greeks

Alexander the Great conquered Egypt in 332BC. Egypt became part of the Greek empire. For over 300 years Greek-speaking pharaohs, including Queen Cleopatra, ruled Egypt. Their capital city was Alexandria in Lower Egypt. Alexandria became a world centre of Greek art, architecture and thought.

Cleopatra and her son Caesarion
This relief carving is on a wall of the temple of Hathor in Alexandria. Cleopatra and Caesarion ruled jointly over Egypt. Here they are making offerings to the Egyptian goddess Hathor.

A mixture of cultures

This is an Egyptian mummy case. The painting on the front is a Roman painting. It is of a young Roman called Artemidorus. He died around AD100 aged about 20.

The Romans

The Romans took control of Egypt in 30BC. Slowly the Egyptians gave up the special way they painted and drew people. They became Christians. In AD640 the Arabs conquered Egypt. They converted the Egyptians to Islam. A small group called Copts kept the Egyptian language and the Christian faith.

Time line

BC

5000 – 3100? Predynastic period. Egyptians stop being hunter-gatherers and become farmers. Craftworkers use stone, copper, clay, wood and leather. Egyptians trade with each other using papyrus boats.

3100 Menes becomes first pharaoh of all Egypt. Hieroglyphic writing begins to record Egyptian history.

3100 – 2649? Capital at Memphis. Trade with Palestine and Nubia.

2649? Beginning of the Old Kingdom.

2630 – 2611? Reign of Zoser. Building of the step pyramid.

2575 – 2465? The age of the true pyramids. Conquest of northern Nubia.

2134? End of the Old Kingdom. Egypt breaks up into different parts.

2040? Mentuhotpe brings different parts of Egypt together. Capital at Thebes. Beginning of the Middle Kingdom.

1991 – 1783? Northern Nubia reconquered. War-like expeditions to Palestine.

1640? End of the Middle Kingdom. Hyksos invaders from Palestine. Hyksos introduce horse-drawn war chariots and iron working.

1550? Egypt re-united as Hyksos driven out. Capital at Thebes. Northern Nubia and parts of Palestine reconquered.

1504 – 1492? Thotmes I creates Egyptian empire by conquering more of Nubia, Palestine and Syria.

1473 – 1458? Hatshepsut becomes Queen with as much power as the pharaohs.

1391 – 1353 Under Amenhotep III, the Egyptian Empire is at its peak.

1353 – 1335? Akhnaton builds new capital at Akhtaton and forces Egyptians to worship only the sun-god Aton. Art becomes more realistic.

1333 – 1323? Rule of Tutankhamon Capital moved to Memphis . The old religions brought back.

1307 – 1070? Pharaohs called Ramses build great monuments Egypt loses control of Palestine and Nubia

1070? End of the New Kingdom.

Priests of Thebes begin ruling Upper Egypt.

770? Nubians conquer most of Upper Egypt.

712? Nubians conquer the rest of Egypt.

664 Necho I drives out Nubians and makes Egypt independent.

525 The Persians conquer Egypt.

332 Alexander the Great of Greece conquers Egypt. The city of Alexandria built.

30 Egypt becomes a province of the Roman Empire.

AD

394 Egypt almost completely Christian.

640 Arabs conquer Egypt. Egyptians converted to Islam.

Glossary

absolute ruler: a king whose power to govern is not limited by law

afterlife: the life of a person's soul after the death of their body

akhet: the season of the Nile flood, August to October

anatomy: the study of bodies, often human

ancestor: person in the family who lived in earlier times

archaeologist: a person who tries to work out what happened in the past by finding and studying old buildings and objects

astronomy: the study of the movement and position of the stars

ba: the part of a person's soul that the Egyptians believed could travel to the Underworld

barter: to trade or bargain with goods

cataract: a large waterfall that prevented boats from passing

charm: object which is believed to have special powers, or bring luck

civilization: a large group of people who have settled in one place and live in the same organized way

delta: the fan-shaped area of muddy land at the place where a river divides and flows into the sea

demotic script: a simplified form of the ancient Egyptian hieratic script, used between 700BC and AD450

dike: ditch or channel cut in the ground

disease: illness

dynasty: a line of rulers belonging to the same family

early period: the time of the first and second Egyptian dynasties (3100–2694(?)BC)

Egyptologist: an expert who studies ancient Egypt

excavation: the careful digging up of buried objects to find information about the past

fertile: the sort of land where plants grow well

Greek period: the time following Alexander the Great's conquest, when the pharaohs spoke Greek and Alexandria became the main centre of Greek civilization (332–30BC)

hieratic script: a simplified form of Egyptian writing which first appeared during the early period

hieroglyphics: a Greek word for an elaborate form of Egyptian writing, used for formal messages such as inscriptions, that used both pictures and sound signs

historian: a person who studies what happened in the past

hunter-gatherers: people who live by hunting for animals, and gathering plants for food

Hyksos: the people who invaded Egypt from Palestine and ruled Egypt during the 15th and 16th dynasties

inscription: a formal message set down in an especially long-lasting form, such as being carved in stone

irrigation: a system of watering crops by channelling water from a river along pipes or ditches

ka: the body-spirit that the Egyptians believed could not survive unless the dead person's body was mummified
kilt: a knee-length skirt worn by men

linen: a strong cloth made from the fibres of the flax plant
Lower Egypt: the part of Egypt that included the Nile Delta and the Nile Valley as far south as Memphis

mastaba: a tomb made of mud bricks and stone in the predynastic or early period
Middle Kingdom: the second great age in Egypt (2040–1640(?)BC)
mummy: a body preserved by drying

New Kingdom: the last great age in Egypt (1550–1070(?)BC), including the days of the Egyptian Empire
nomarch: the Greek word for the governor of a nome, which was a small Egyptian province

oasis: an isolated fertile area in a dry region, where crops can be grown
Old Kingdom: the first great age in Egypt (2649–2134(?)BC), when most of the pyramids were built

papyrus: a reed which grew in Nile swamps; the shoots were a luxury food, the stems were woven together to make boats; the pith was cut into strips which stuck together when they were beaten. Papyrus sheets were used for writing on
peret: the season of planting and fresh growth, from November to February
pharaoh: a king of Egypt

predynastic period: the time before Egyptian history began

regent: someone who rules on behalf of a child who is too young to come to the throne
relief: a picture carved in a flat surface

sacrifice: thing or person which is given up (or killed), often as an offering to a god
scribe: an official, a secretary or clerk whose work involved writing
scroll: several sheets of papyrus joined into a rolled strip
shemu: the dry season from March to August, when crops ripened and were harvested
shrine: a holy place where believers keep an object that they link closely with a god or spirit
site: place or position, especially where something of historic interest happened or can be seen
step pyramid: a tomb or temple built up of layers, each layer being smaller than the one below

true pyramid: a tomb or pyramid with a square base and four outside walls in the form of triangles that meet at the top

Underworld: the world of the afterlife, where the Egyptians believed that the sun-god came back to life each night
Upper Egypt: the part of Egypt that included the Nile Valley from Memphis, south to the first cataract

vizier: an Arabic word for the scribe who was the chief advisor to the pharaoh

Index